*Rick Steves*®

# NORTHERN EUROPEAN CRUISE PORTS

Rick Steves with Cameron Hewitt

# CONTENTS

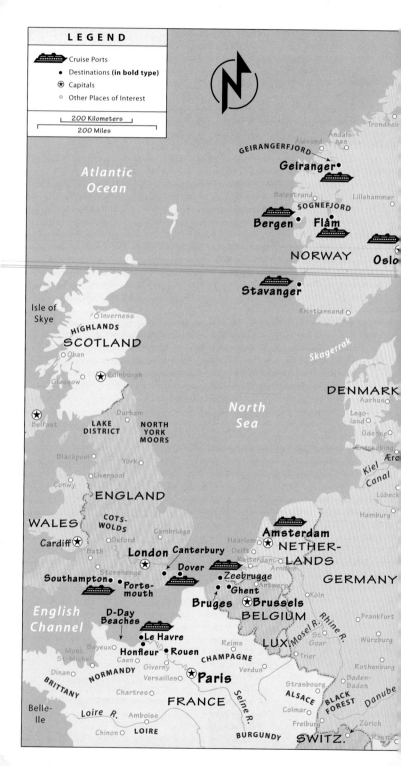

# Northern Europe

SWEDEN

FINLAND

Savonlinna

*Lake Ladoga*

St. Petersburg

Peterhof

RUSSIA

*Gulf of Bothnia*

Turku

Helsinki

*Gulf of Finland*

Tallinn

ESTONIA

Uppsala

Stockholm

Saaremaa

Göteborg

Visby

Gotland

Riga

LATVIA

Kalmar

Växjö

Öland

LITHUANIA

Klaipeda

Vilnius

Minsk

*Kattegat*

*Baltic Sea*

Copenhagen

Malmö

Rønne

Bornholm

Gdynia

Gdańsk

Malbork

RUSSIA

BELARUS

Warnemünde

Rostock

Poznań

Toruń

*Elbe R.*

Berlin

Warsaw

Wittenberg

POLAND

Leipzig

Dresden

*Oder R.*

Auschwitz

*Vistula R.*

Kraków

L'viv

UKRAINE

Prague

CZECH REPUBLIC

Nürnberg

Český Krumlov

Brno

TATRA MTNS.

Levoča

SLOVAKIA

Munich

Melk

Bratislava

Eger

BAVARIA

Salzburg

Hallstatt

Vienna

Budapest

ROMANIA

Füssen

Innsbruck

AUSTRIA

*Lake Balaton*

HUNGARY

Sighişoara

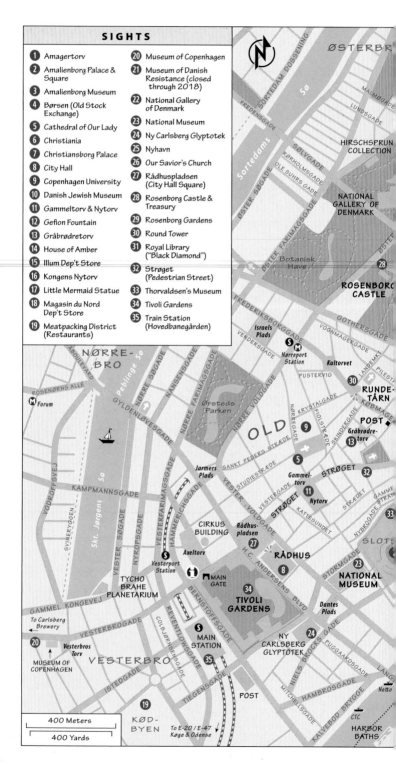

## SIGHTS

1. Amagertorv
2. Amalienborg Palace & Square
3. Amalienborg Museum
4. Børsen (Old Stock Exchange)
5. Cathedral of Our Lady
6. Christiania
7. Christiansborg Palace
8. City Hall
9. Copenhagen University
10. Danish Jewish Museum
11. Gammeltorv & Nytorv
12. Gefion Fountain
13. Gråbrødretorv
14. House of Amber
15. Illum Dep't Store
16. Kongens Nytorv
17. Little Mermaid Statue
18. Magasin du Nord Dep't Store
19. Meatpacking District (Restaurants)
20. Museum of Copenhagen
21. Museum of Danish Resistance (closed through 2018)
22. National Gallery of Denmark
23. National Museum
24. Ny Carlsberg Glyptotek
25. Nyhavn
26. Our Savior's Church
27. Rådhuspladsen (City Hall Square)
28. Rosenborg Castle & Treasury
29. Rosenborg Gardens
30. Round Tower
31. Royal Library ("Black Diamond")
32. Strøget (Pedestrian Street)
33. Thorvaldsen's Museum
34. Tivoli Gardens
35. Train Station (Hovedbanegården)

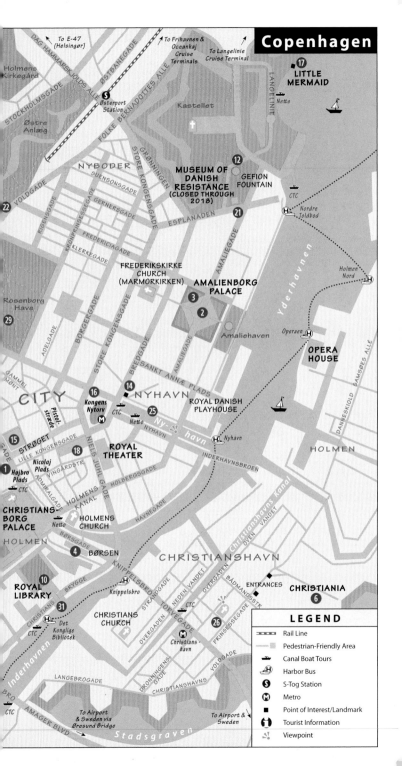

# Copenhagen

**To E-47 (Helsingør)**
**To Frihavnen & Oceankaj Cruise Terminals**
**To Langelinie Cruise Terminal**

⑰ LITTLE MERMAID

ØSTBANEGADE

DAG HAMMARSKJØLDS ALLÉ

Holmens Kirkegård

STOCKHOLMSGADE

Ⓢ Østerport Station

FOLKE BERNADOTTES ALLÉ

Kastellet

LANGELINIE

*Netto*

Østre Anlæg

NYBODER

SUENSONSGADE

GRØNNINGEN

STORE KONGENSGADE

MUSEUM OF DANISH RESISTANCE (CLOSED THROUGH 2018)

⑫ GEFION FOUNTAIN

CTC

② WOLDGADE

RIGENSGADE

GERNERSGADE

KRONPRINSESSEGADE

KØNIGSGADE

ESPLANADEN

㉑

Nordre Toldbod Ⓗ

FREDERICIAGADE

KLERKEGADE

Yderhavnen

Rosenborg Have

ⓐⓦ

ADELGADE

BORGERGADE

STORE KONGENSGADE

BREDGADE

FREDERIKSKIRKE CHURCH (MARMORKIRKEN)

③

② AMALIENBORG PALACE

AMALIEGADE

Holmen Nord Ⓗ

Amaliehaven

Operaen Ⓗ

OPERA HOUSE

GAMMEL MØNT

CITY

SANKT ANNÆ PLADS

DANNESKIOLD SAMSØES ALLÉ

Pistol-stræde

⑯ Kongens Nytorv

CTC

⑭ NYHAVN

Ⓜ

㉕ *Netto*

ROYAL DANISH PLAYHOUSE

⑮ STRØGET

LILLE KONGENSGADE

⑱

NIELS JUHLS GADE

Ny havn

HOLMEN

① Højbro Plads

Nicolaj Plads

VINGÅRDSTR

ROYAL THEATER

NYHAVN

Nyhavn Ⓗ

INDERHAVNSBROEN

ADMIRALGADE

HOLMENS KANAL

HOLBERGSGADE

CHRISTIANS BORG PALACE

HOLMEN

*Netto*

HOLMENS CHURCH

HAVNEGADE

BØRSGADE

④ BØRSEN

Christianshavns Kanal

OVEN VANDET

KNIPPELSBRODGADE

CHRISTIANSHAVN

⑩ ROYAL LIBRARY

CHRISTIANS BRYGGE

Ⓗ

Knippelsbro

STRANDGADE

OVERGADEN NEDEN VANDET

OVERGADEN OVEN VANDET

BÅDMANDSSTR

■ ENTRANCES

CHRISTIANIA ⑥

㉛

Det Kongelige Bibliotek

CTC

CHRISTIANS CHURCH

TORVEGADE

CTC

㉖

PRINSESSEGADE

Inderhavnen

LANGEBROGADE

DRONNINGENS GADE

Christians-havn

VOLDGADE

BRO

CTC

AMAGER BLVD

CHRISTIANSHAVNS

**To Airport & Sweden via Øresund Bridge**

**To Airport & Sweden**

*Stadsgraven*

## LEGEND

| | |
|---|---|
| ▭▭▭ | Rail Line |
| ▬ | Pedestrian-Friendly Area |
| ⚓ | Canal Boat Tours |
| Ⓗ | Harbor Bus |
| Ⓢ | S-Tog Station |
| Ⓜ | Metro |
| ■ | Point of Interest/Landmark |
| ✝ | Tourist Information |
| ⌃! | Viewpoint |

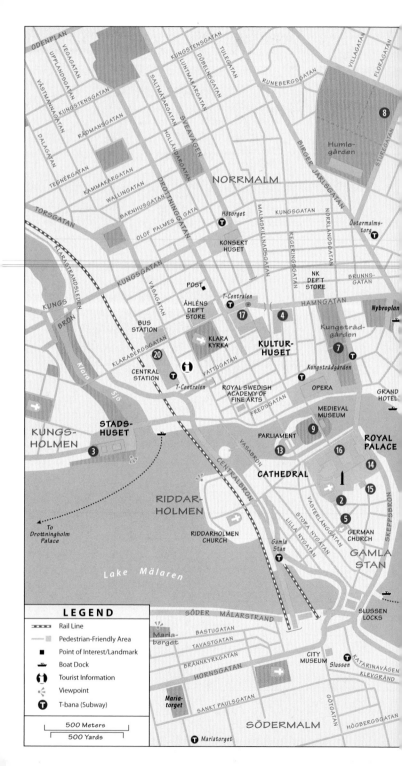

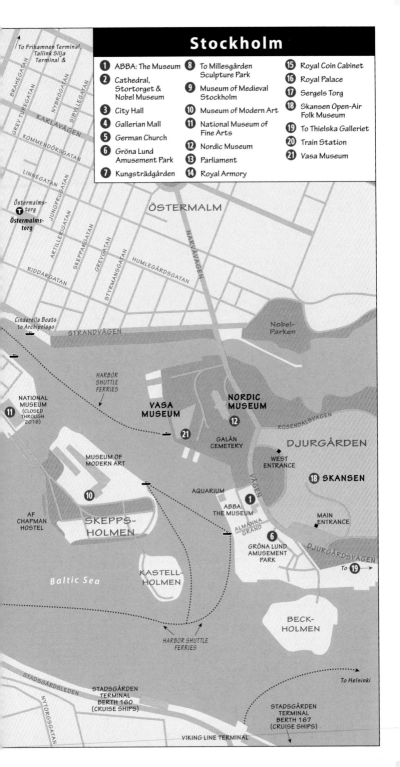

# Stockholm

1. ABBA: The Museum
2. Cathedral, Stortorget & Nobel Museum
3. City Hall
4. Gallerian Mall
5. German Church
6. Gröna Lund Amusement Park
7. Kungsträdgården
8. To Millesgården Sculpture Park
9. Museum of Medieval Stockholm
10. Museum of Modern Art
11. National Museum of Fine Arts
12. Nordic Museum
13. Parliament
14. Royal Armory
15. Royal Coin Cabinet
16. Royal Palace
17. Sergels Torg
18. Skansen Open-Air Folk Museum
19. To Thielska Galleriet
20. Train Station
21. Vasa Museum

To Frihamnen Terminal, Tallink Silja Terminal &

BRAHEGATAN
NYBROGATAN
SIBYLLEGATAN
GREV TUREGATAN
KARLAVÄGEN
KOMMENDÖRSGATAN
LINNÉGATAN

Östermalms-torg
Östermalms-torg

ÖSTERMALM

JUNGFRUGATAN
ARTILLERIGATAN
SKEPPARGATAN
GREVGATAN
STYRMANSGATAN
NARVAVÄGEN
HUMLEGÅRDSGATAN

RIDDARGATAN

Cinderella Boats to Archipelago

STRANDVÄGEN

Nobel-Parken

HARBOR SHUTTLE FERRIES

11 NATIONAL MUSEUM (CLOSED THROUGH 2016)

VASA MUSEUM
21

NORDIC MUSEUM
12

ROSENDALSVÄGEN

DJURGÅRDEN

GALÄN CEMETERY

WEST ENTRANCE

18 SKANSEN

MUSEUM OF MODERN ART
10

AQUARIUM

ABBA: THE MUSEUM
1

MAIN ENTRANCE

AF CHAPMAN HOSTEL

SKEPPS-HOLMEN

ALMÄNNA GRAND

GRÖNA LUND AMUSEMENT PARK
6

DJURGÅRDSVÄGEN

To 19

Baltic Sea

KASTELL-HOLMEN

BECK-HOLMEN

HARBOR SHUTTLE FERRIES

STADSGÅRDSLEDEN
NYTORGSGATAN

STADSGÅRDEN TERMINAL BERTH 160 (CRUISE SHIPS)

To Helsinki

STADSGÅRDEN TERMINAL BERTH 167 (CRUISE SHIPS)

VIKING LINE TERMINAL

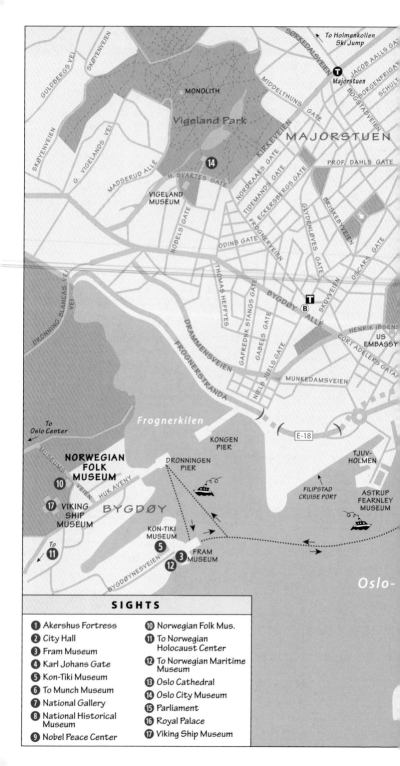

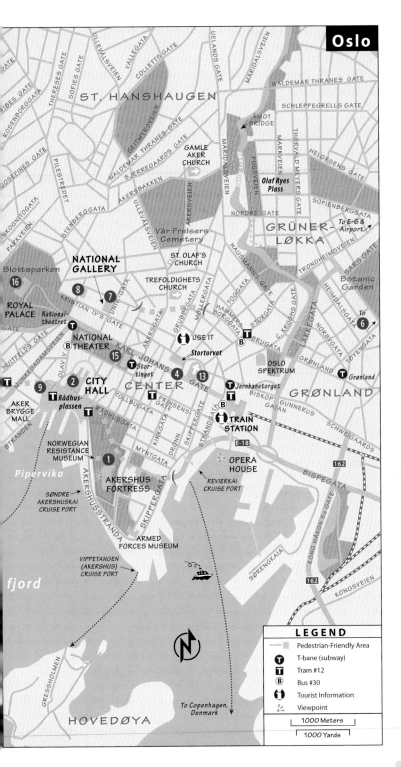

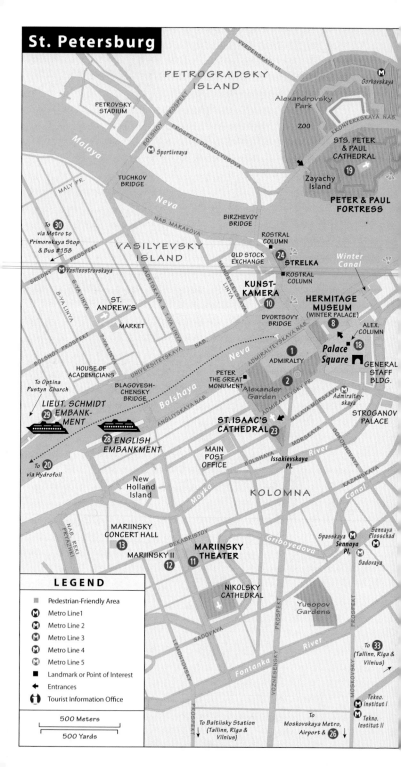

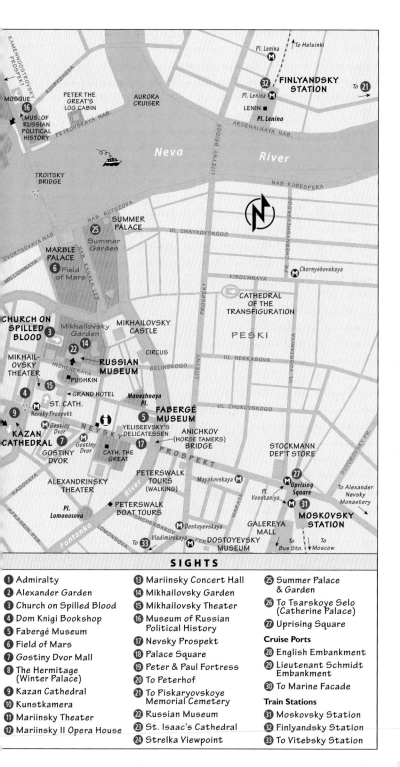

## SIGHTS

1. Admiralty
2. Alexander Garden
3. Church on Spilled Blood
4. Dom Knigi Bookshop
5. Fabergé Museum
6. Field of Mars
7. Gostiny Dvor Mall
8. The Hermitage (Winter Palace)
9. Kazan Cathedral
10. Kunstkamera
11. Mariinsky Theater
12. Mariinsky II Opera House

13. Mariinsky Concert Hall
14. Mikhailovsky Garden
15. Mikhailovsky Theater
16. Museum of Russian Political History
17. Nevsky Prospekt
18. Palace Square
19. Peter & Paul Fortress
20. To Peterhof
21. To Piskaryovskoye Memorial Cemetery
22. Russian Museum
23. St. Isaac's Cathedral
24. Strelka Viewpoint

25. Summer Palace & Garden
26. To Tsarskoye Selo (Catherine Palace)
27. Uprising Square

**Cruise Ports**

28. English Embankment
29. Lieutenant Schmidt Embankment
30. To Marine Facade

**Train Stations**

31. Moskovsky Station
32. Finlyandsky Station
33. To Vitebsky Station

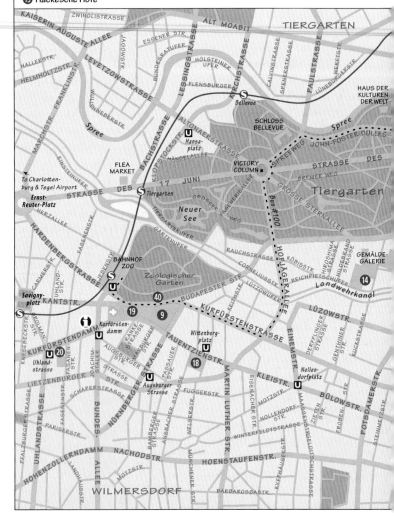

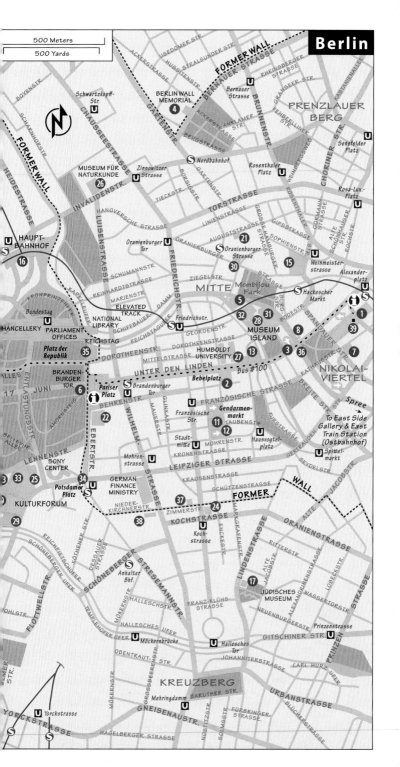

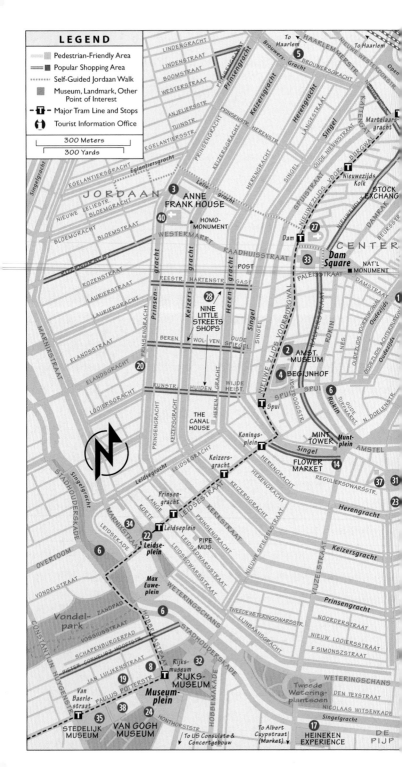

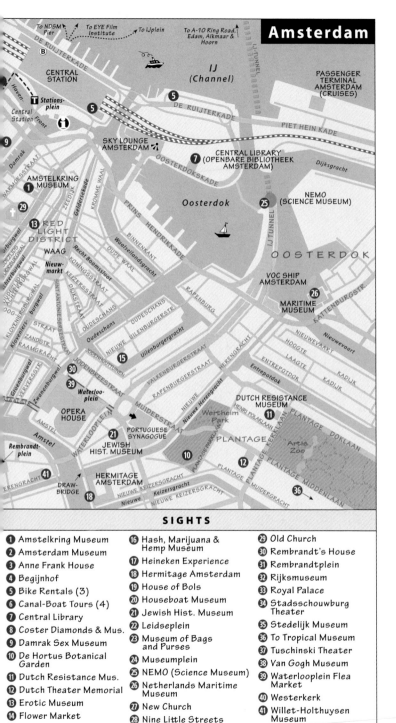

# Amsterdam

## SIGHTS

1. Amstelkring Museum
2. Amsterdam Museum
3. Anne Frank House
4. Begijnhof
5. Bike Rentals (3)
6. Canal-Boat Tours (4)
7. Central Library
8. Coster Diamonds & Mus.
9. Damrak Sex Museum
10. De Hortus Botanical Garden
11. Dutch Resistance Mus.
12. Dutch Theater Memorial
13. Erotic Museum
14. Flower Market
15. Gassan Diamonds
16. Hash, Marijuana & Hemp Museum
17. Heineken Experience
18. Hermitage Amsterdam
19. House of Bols
20. Houseboat Museum
21. Jewish Hist. Museum
22. Leidseplein
23. Museum of Bags and Purses
24. Museumplein
25. NEMO (Science Museum)
26. Netherlands Maritime Museum
27. New Church
28. Nine Little Streets Shopping District
29. Old Church
30. Rembrandt's House
31. Rembrandtplein
32. Rijksmuseum
33. Royal Palace
34. Stadsschouwburg Theater
35. Stedelijk Museum
36. To Tropical Museum
37. Tuschinski Theater
38. Van Gogh Museum
39. Waterlooplein Flea Market
40. Westerkerk
41. Willet-Holthuysen Museum

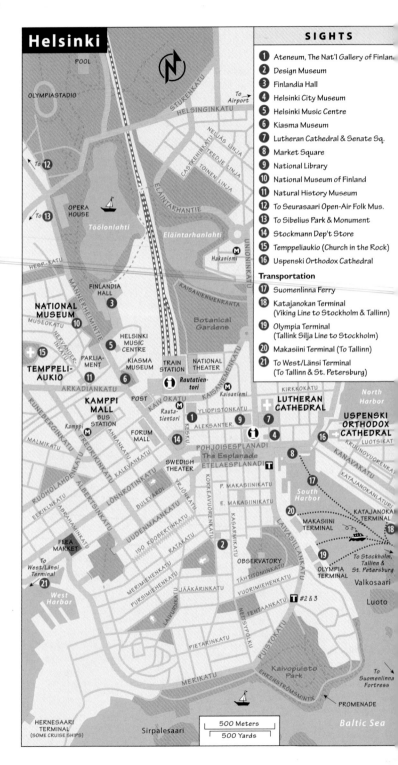

# Helsinki

## SIGHTS

1. Ateneum, The Nat'l Gallery of Finland
2. Design Museum
3. Finlandia Hall
4. Helsinki City Museum
5. Helsinki Music Centre
6. Kiasma Museum
7. Lutheran Cathedral & Senate Sq.
8. Market Square
9. National Library
10. National Museum of Finland
11. Natural History Museum
12. To Seurasaari Open-Air Folk Mus.
13. To Sibelius Park & Monument
14. Stockmann Dep't Store
15. Temppeliaukio (Church in the Rock)
16. Uspenski Orthodox Cathedral

### Transportation

17. Suomenlinna Ferry
18. Katajanokan Terminal (Viking Line to Stockholm & Tallinn)
19. Olympia Terminal (Tallink Silja Line to Stockholm)
20. Makasiini Terminal (To Tallinn)
21. To West/Länsi Terminal (To Tallinn & St. Petersburg)

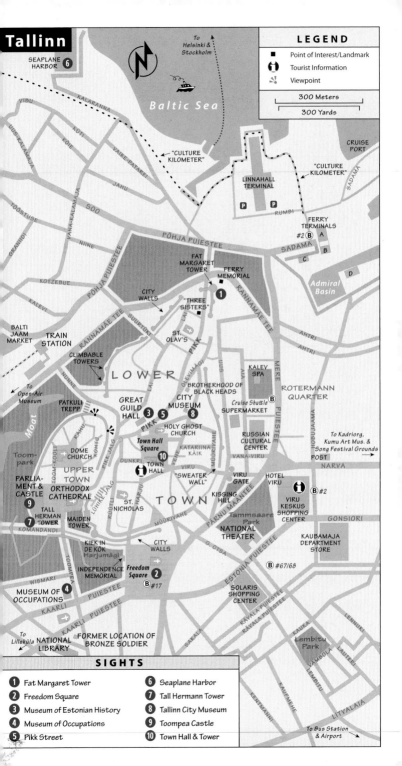

# Tallinn

SEAPLANE HARBOR 6

VIBU

KALARANNA

KUTI

VAIKE-PATAREI

SOO

JAHU

To Helsinki & Stockholm

N

Baltic Sea

"CULTURE KILOMETER"

CRUISE PORT

SADAMA

LINNAHALL TERMINAL

"CULTURE KILOMETER"

P P

RUMBI

FERRY TERMINALS

#2 🅱 A

SADAMA

B

C

Admiral Basin

D

LÜÜSI-KALAMAJA

KOIE

TÖÖSTUSE

GRANIIDI

KOTZEBUE

POHJA PUIESTEE

NIINE

PÕHJA PUIESTEE

FAT MARGARET TOWER

FERRY MEMORIAL

1

RANNAMÄE TEE

KALEVI

CITY WALLS

"THREE SISTERS"

AHTRI

AHTRI

BALTI JAAM MARKET

TRAIN STATION

RANNAMÄE TEE

NUNNE

CLIMBABLE TOWERS

L O W E R

ST. OLAV'S

SUURTÜKI

LAI

VAIMU

PIKK

BROTHERHOOD OF BLACK HEADS

UUS

AIA

KALEV SPA

MERE PUIESTEE

ROTERMANN QUARTER

HOBUJAAMA

To Open-Air Museum

PATKULI TREPP

RAHU

GREAT GUILD HALL

CITY MUSEUM

3 5 8

Cruise Shuttle SUPERMARKET

🅱

To Kadriorg, Kumu Art Mus. & Song Festival Grounds →

Moat

TOOM-KOOLI

DOME CHURCH

PIKK JALG

PIKK

HOLY GHOST CHURCH

Town Hall Square

10

KATARIINA KÄIK

MÜÜRIVAHE

VENE

RUSSIAN CULTURAL CENTER

VANA-VIRU

POST

NARVA

Toom-park

UPPER TOWN

TOOM-RÜÜTLI

PARLIA-MENT & CASTLE

9

PIKK JALG

LÜHIKE JALG

RÜÜTLI

ORTHODOX CATHEDRAL

DUNKRI

HARJU

TOWN HALL

🛈

VIRU

"SWEATER WALL"

VIRU GATE

KISSING HILL

HOTEL VIRU

🛈 🅱 #2

VIRU KESKUS SHOPPING CENTER

GONSIORI

TALL HERMAN TOWER

7

ST. NICHOLAS

T O W N

MÜÜRIVAHE

PÄRNU MAANTEE

Tammsaare Park

KAUBAMAJA DEPARTMENT STORE

MAIDEN TOWER

KOMANDANDI

TOOMPEA

KIEK IN DE KÖK Harjumägi

CITY WALLS

NATIONAL THEATER

G. OTSA

WISMARI

INDEPENDENCE MEMORIAL

Freedom Square

2

🅱 #17

ESTONIA PUIESTEE

🅱 #67/68

SOLARIS SHOPPING CENTER

RÄVALA PUIESTEE

LEMBITU PÄIESTEE

Lembitu Park

KAARLI

MUSEUM OF OCCUPATIONS

4

KAARLI PUIESTEE

FORMER LOCATION OF BRONZE SOLDIER

SAKALA

RÄVALA PUIESTEE

KAUKA

LAULU

LAUTERI

LEMBITU

VAMBOLA

KAUPMEHE

RENTMEISTRI

LITVALALA

To Lilleküla

NATIONAL LIBRARY

To Bus Station & Airport →

## SIGHTS

1 Fat Margaret Tower

2 Freedom Square

3 Museum of Estonian History

4 Museum of Occupations

5 Pikk Street

6 Seaplane Harbor

7 Tall Hermann Tower

8 Tallinn City Museum

9 Toompea Castle

10 Town Hall & Tower